£7.99

Continued on page 11...

Introducing the *amazing* wall-crawling, web-slinging, wise cracking super-hero...

SPIDER-MAN

POWER RANKING:

STRENGTH:	12
SPEED:	10
INTELLIGENCE:	13
AGILITY:	14
POWERS:	14

NAME: Peter Parker
HEIGHT: 5' 10"
WEIGHT: 165 lbs
EQUIPMENT: Web-spinners, spider-tracers, spider signal.
POWERS / ABILITIES: Super-human strength and agility, wall-crawling, spider-sense and an accelerated healing ability.

FACT FILE!

SPIDEY FACT:

Spider-Man can lift up to 10 tons, that's the same weight as a small elephant!

SPIDEY FACT:

Spidey is 15 times more agile than a regular human being. He can also leap up to 30 feet in a single jump!

SPIDEY FACT:

Spidey uses his spider-sense as an early warning system. It alerts him to all forms of danger.

WEB SHOOTERS

Peter used his science skills to create these awesome web-slingers. These devices fire a thin strand of "web-fluid" approximately 60 ft long. Each web-spinner can hold up to 10,000 yards of webbing!

THE ORIGINS OF... SPIDER-MAN

WHEN SHY HIGH SCHOOL STUDENT PETER PARKER WAS BITTEN BY AN IRRADIATED SPIDER, HE GAINED AMAZING POWERS.

AT FIRST HE USED THESE ABILITIES TO BECOME A TV STAR.

BUT WHEN HIS BELOVED UNCLE BEN WAS KILLED BY A BURGLAR, HE REALISED THERE WAS A MUCH BETTER WAY TO USE THEM.

HE BECAME THE AMAZING SPIDER-MAN - DEDICATING HIS LIFE TO COMBATING EVIL AND HELPING THOSE IN NEED!

THE INVINCIBLE IRON MAN

Tony Stark, committed businessman, inventor and now... Super Hero. Read on to find out more about the man behind the metal.

REAL NAME:
TONY STARK
HEIGHT: 6' 1"
WEIGHT: 225 LBS
EYES: BLUE
HAIR: BLACK
POWERS / ABILITIES:
HIGHLY ADVANCED
BATTLE SUIT

DID YOU KNOW?

Stark's cover story is that Iron Man is his personal bodyguard and Stark Industries' company mascot!

POWER RANKING:

STRENGTH:	14
SPEED:	12
INTELLIGENCE:	12
AGILITY:	10
POWERS:	15

VOICE CONVERTER

COMMS COMPUTER

SHIELD GENERATOR

PARTICLE BEAN EMITTERS

Each of his gloves feature a palm mounted particle beam emitter which is so powerful it can blast through 4 feet of concrete and liquefy most metals.

TACTICAL DATA DISPLAY:

Iron Man's eyepieces provide Stark with critical information such as fuel levels, altitude and incoming threats. The optical sensors are capable of ultra violet, x-ray and infrared vision!

UNI-BEAM PROJECTOR:

A powerful chest mounted particle beam emitter than can fire destructive forms of light energy.

A modern day suit of armour... Constructed from lightweight titanium alloy and capable of absorbing a bazooka blast, Stark's armoured suit is not just a costume to mask his identity.

THE ORIGINS OF... IRON MAN

WHILST FIELD-TESTING HIS LATEST INVENTION, BILLIONAIRE WEAPONS CREATOR TONY STARK WAS CAPTURED BY TERRORISTS.

HIS CAPTORS ORDERED HIM TO BUILD THEM A MIGHTY WEAPON.

BUT INSTEAD HE SECRETLY BUILT A MECHANCIAL SUIT OF ARMOUR STRONG ENOUGH TO FREE HIM FROM HIS CAPTORS.

RETURNING TO AMERICA, TONY REDESIGNED HIS SUIT AND VOWED TO USE IT TO HELP THOSE IN NEED AS THE INVINCIBLE IRON MAN!

...Continued from page 8

Continued on page 17...

THE HULK

Who is this super strong, green skinned 7-foot-tall monster? Is he really a menace or simply misunderstood?

REAL NAME:
DR BRUCE BANNER
HEIGHT: 7'
WEIGHT: 1040 LBS
EYES: GREEN
HAIR: GREEN
POWERS | ABILITIES:
SUPER STRENGTH AND REGENERATION

POWER RANKING:

STRENGTH:	20
SPEED:	14
INTELLIGENCE:	5
AGILITY:	7
POWERS:	18

LEAPS & BOUNDS

The Hulk uses his superhuman strong leg muscles to leap great distances - he can leap up to 3 miles in a single jump!

BULLET PROOF

The Hulk's skin is so tough even armour - piercing bullets ricochet off of him!

HULK SMASH!

The Hulk can floor his foes simply by smashing his hands together. This creates an almighty sonic boom that knocks down his enemies and disorientates them. **BOOOOOM!**

ANGER MANAGEMENT

Dr. Bruce Banner transforms into the Hulk when he gets angry, anxious or stressed. Once transformed, the angrier Hulk gets, the stronger he becomes.

HULK IS THE STRONGEST ONE THERE IS!

THE ORIGINS OF... THE HULK

DR. BRUCE BANNER WORKED FOR THE US MILITARY HELPING THEM TO DEVELOP A NEW EXPERIMENTAL WEAPON...

...THE GAMMA BOMB!

MY BOMB BETTER WORK BANNER -- OR ELSE!

BUT ON THE DAY OF THE FIRST TEST, HIS LIFE CHANGED FOREVER!

ARGH!

DUE TO A FREAK ACCIDENT, DR. BANNER WAS CAUGHT IN THE EXPLODING BOMB'S BLAST.

AS THE SMOKE CLEARED THE BOMB'S EFFECTS BECAME APPARENT...

BANNER HAD BEEN CHANGED INTO A GREEN-SKINNED, SUPER STRONG, 7-FOOT-TALL MONSTER.

HE HAD BECOME THE HULK!

KANG THE CONQUEROR

He's an expert in time travel, a skilled strategist, a veteran of armed and unarmed combat and has mastered the future's advanced technologies. *Marvel Fans,* meet the almighty...

KANG THE CONQUEROR...

NAME: NATHANIEL RICHARDS
HEIGHT: 6'3"
WEIGHT: 230 lbs
POWERS / ABILITIES: TRAVEL THROUGH AND THE MANIPULATION OF TIME. EXPERT STRATEGIST IN ARMED AND UNARMED COMBAT
OCCUPATION: CONQUEROR!
BORN: 31ST CENTURY EARTH

ANTI-AGEING

Kang ages at a slightly slower rate than normal human beings.

KANG'S ARMADA

Every conqueror needs an army and Kang's no exception. He commands his vast armada of warriors from across the galaxy. He uses robots such as his Growing-Man stimuloids, packed with the "Growth Pollen" from the world of Kosmos. This causes them to grow in size and strengthen by absorbing kinetic energy.

POWER RANKING:

STRENGTH:	9
SPEED:	15
INTELLIGENCE:	13
AGILITY:	11
POWERS:	14

WEAPONARY

Wow, Kang certainly means business with this arsenal of fancy weaponry. Check out these futuristic firearms he carries!

- ☠ Anti-matter defense screen generator
- ☠ Vibration ray projector
- ☠ Electromagnetic field-amplifier
- ☠ Neutrino tipped missile launcher (hand-gun size)
- ☠ Electrical paralysis generator
- ☠ Nerve gas sprayer
- ☠ Molecular expander

BODY ARMOUR

This isn't any ordinary suit of armour! Check out some of its awesome features:

- ☠ It enables Kang to lift up to 5 tons.
- ☠ It can project a 20-foot force field, which can even shield him from a direct nuclear strike.
- ☠ The suit has a self-contained atmosphere, food supply and waste disposal system, handy for long journeys!
- ☠ The armour's gauntlets feature two massively powerful anti-graviton particle projectors.

...Continued from page 14

Continued on page 26...

MARVEL
MASTERPIECE
Grab your pens or pencils and add a plash of colour to this picture of our Super Heroes!

Kang's

I have travelled through the wormholes in time to bring you these dastardly teasers, but be warned I'm far more intelligent than you think. Good luck, you'll need it... *Ha-haa!*

1 SNACK ATTACK

TEST 1

Hulk has got the hunger! Can you spot 8 packets of Deja Chew just like this one? Beware of imitations!

DEJA CHEW A LIGHT TASTING CRISPY SNACK POTATO CHIPS

2 CODE BREAKER

TEST 2

Crack the code to work out what the heroes need to destroy in order to foil Kang's master plan.

CODE:

=A	=B	=C	=D
=E	=F	=G	=H
=I	=J	=K	=L
=M	=N	=O	=P
=Q	=R	=S	=T
=U	=V	=W	=X
=Y	=Z		

DESTROY THE

Conundrums

3 ALTERED IMAGE

TEST 3
Time travel seems to have made some changes to Spidey, Hulk and Iron Man. Can you spot 8 differences.

ORIGINAL

4 KANG'S THRONE

TEST 4
Look at this picture of Kang on his throne. Can you spot 5 items that shouldn't be there?

...Continued from page 22

27

31

MARVEL® MEGA WORDSEARCH

HEADS UP, MARVEL MANIACS! WE'VE CREATED A MEGA WORD SEARCH BASED ON THE AVENGER'S RUN-IN WITH KANG. SEE IF YOU CAN FIND ALL THE HIDDEN WORDS!

REVERSIVE

TIME TRAVEL SPIDER-MAN DEJA CHEW CAVEMEN

IRON MAN CRYSTALARIUM BEEF JERKY POTATO CHIP

HULK KANG QUARK

MUCHO MUNCHO NHILATOR

```
I Y I T G P I H C O T A T O P
B S S I N I H I L A T O R G V
R U U M M C N C W K P Y A S X
E D Q E U S R R J X M K N X U
V J T T C P S Y K S Q R A L P
E E Q R H N I S V E Y E M U O
R M U A O E D T C T B J R H W
S Q A V M X R A G D W F E K I
I E R E U K U L N D F E D C R
V C K L N G N A A Q Q E I A O
E D A Y C W L R K Z D B P V N
T W I V H B E I N O K L S E M
P P O J O A S U D D V Y U D M
A Z W H K G G M F H P V U E A
V I G L L D E J A C H E W N V
```

ANSWERS ON PAGE 62!

33

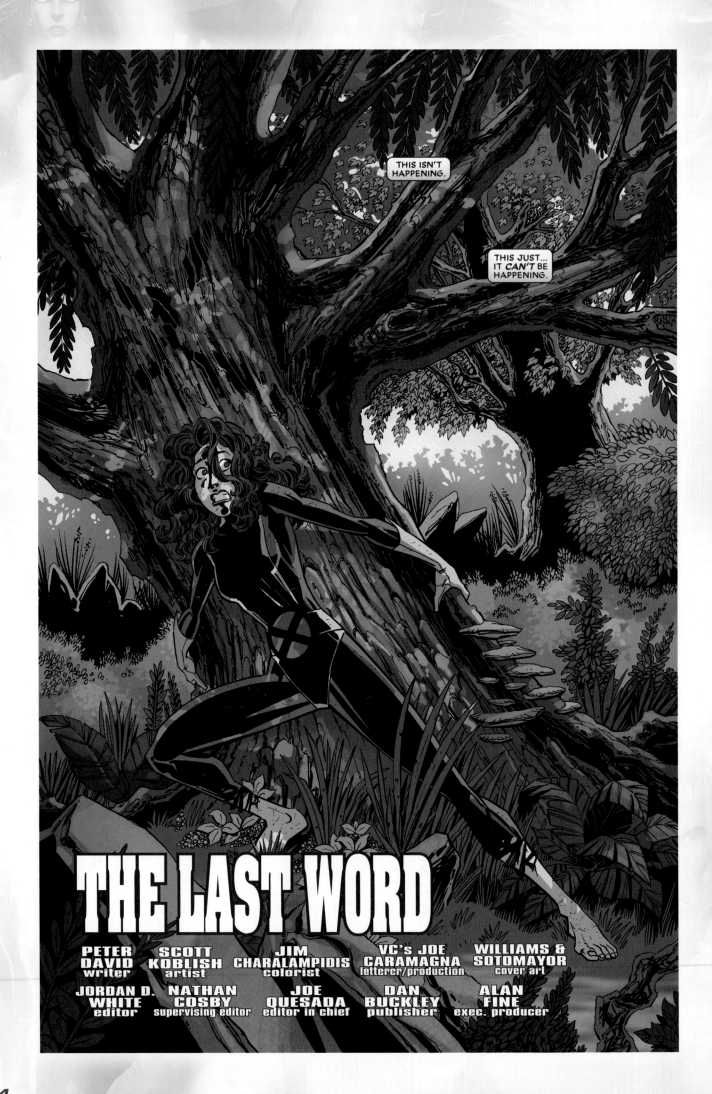

Continued on page 43...

WOLVERINE

You'd have to go a *long way* to find two less likely friends than Wolverine and Kitty Pryde! Read on to find out about these two mis-matched, mutant team-mates!

Wolverine is over 200-years-old, making him the X-Men's oldest team member. His long life is due to his mutant healing factor, which allows him to recover from any injury and slows his ageing.

At some point in his past, Wolverine was used as a guinea pig in a secret experiment called Weapon X. The Weapon X scientists bonded the indestructible metal adamantium to his bones, making them impossible to break.

REAL NAME:
JAMES HOWLETT / LOGAN
HEIGHT: 5' 3"
WEIGHT: 300 LBS
EYES: BLUE
HAIR: BLACK
POWERS / ABILITIES:
MUTANT HEALING FACTOR, CLAWS AND AN INDESTRUCTIBLE ADAMANTIUM SKELETON.

POWER RANKING:

STRENGTH:	8
SPEED:	8
INTELLIGENCE:	9
AGILITY:	8
POWERS:	12

ROOOOAARR!!

LEADER OF THE PACK

Thanks to years of training, Wolverine is an expert hand-to-hand fighter and master of many forms of martial arts.

DID YOU KNOW?

He also has an enhanced sense of taste, smell and hearing allowing him to track down opponents with ease.

SLICE N' DICE

Wolverine's claws are also coated in adamantium, making them strong enough to cut through any metal.

KITTY PRYDE

One of the X-Men's youngest members, Kitty has the mutant power to phase her body, allowing her to pass through solid surfaces like a ghost. She can also phase other objects or people she touches.

POWER RANKING:

STRENGTH:	9
SPEED:	10
INTELLIGENCE:	12
AGILITY:	10
POWERS:	14

REAL NAME:
KITTY PRYDE
HEIGHT: 5' 6"
WEIGHT: 110 LBS
EYES: BROWN
HAIR: BROWN
POWERS / ABILITIES:
PHASING, MARTIAL ARTS AND AN EXTENSIVE KNOWLEDGE OF COMPUTER PROGRAMMING.

X TAUGHT BY THE BEST

Kitty is an accomplished martial artist and has been taught many different styles of fighting by her team-mate and mentor, Wolverine.

If Kitty passes through electrical equipment when she is intangible, her body will cause the machinery to short circuit.

X DID YOU KNOW?

When kitty is phased with the air around her she becomes weightless and gains the ability to fly.

WOLVERINE

WOLVERINE

ORIGINAL

Listen up, gang!
Want to learn how to draw me?
Copy this picture, square-by-square, into the empty box below, then grab your pencils and add a splash of colour!

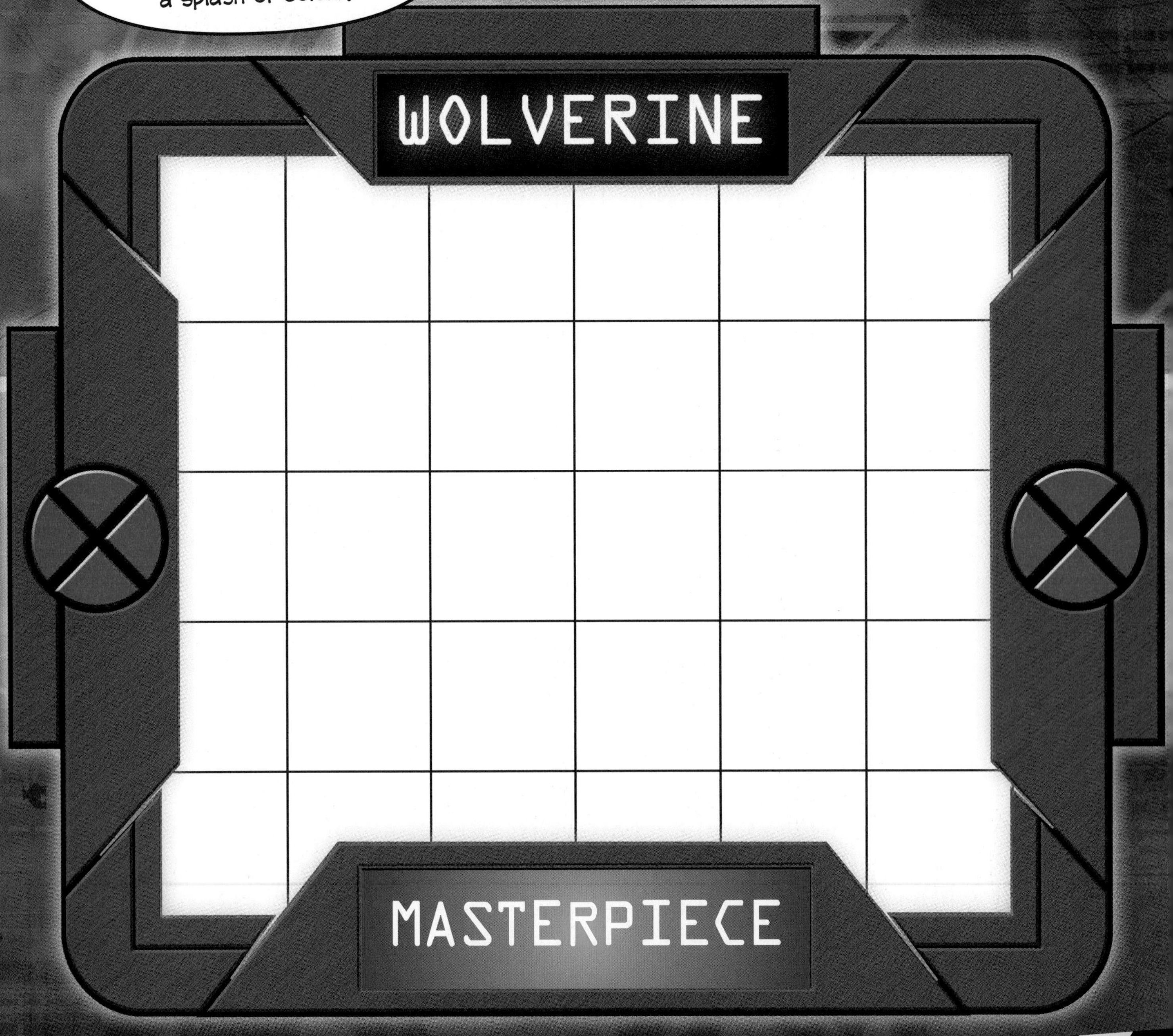

WOLVERINE

MASTERPIECE

...Continued from page 39

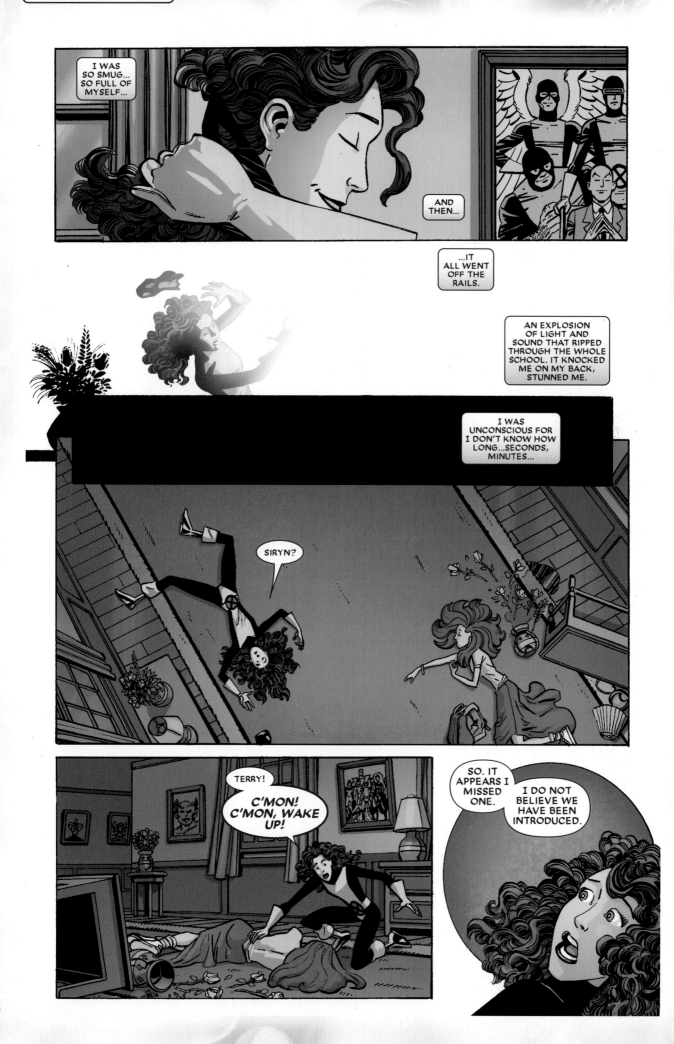

Continued on page 48...

X-Mansion Escape!

Magneto seems to have taken control of Wolverine and he's out to get Kitty! She can't phase, so you need to help her escape the X-Men Mansion - but be quick, he's closing in on her!

DANGER ROOM
START

GROUND FLOOR
LEVEL 1

4 FIND THE MAIN EXIT

1 LIFT TO BASEMENT

5 EXIT

BASEMENT 1
LEVEL -1

RUN TO THE WOODS!

FINISH

3 LIFT TO GROUND FLOOR

2

ANSWERS ON PAGE 62!

...Continued from page 46

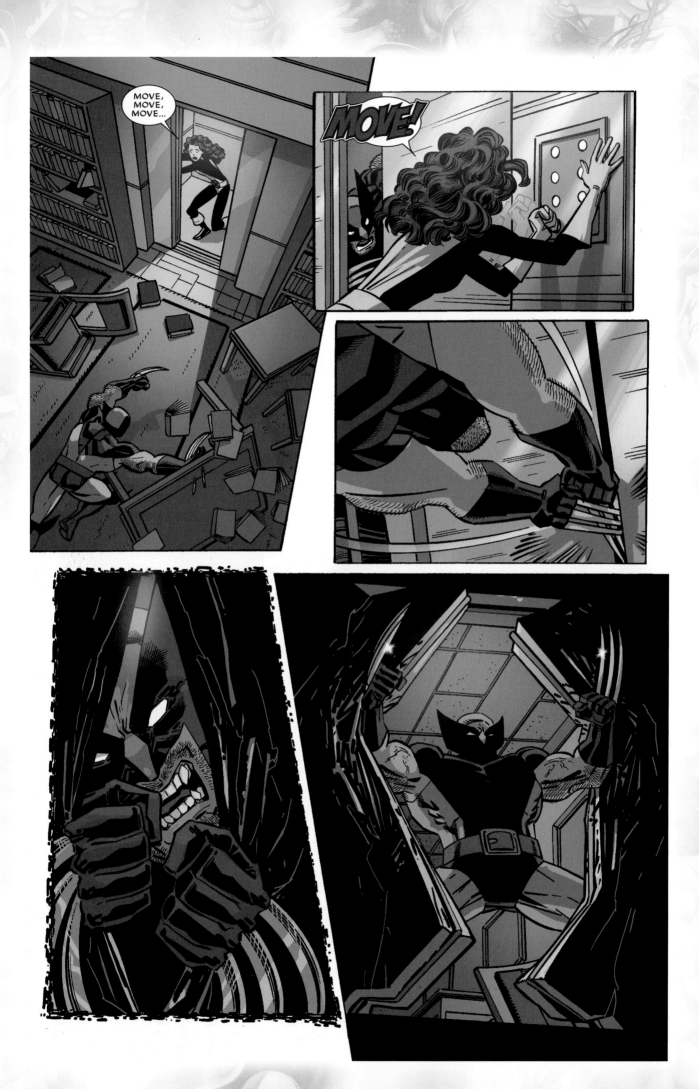

Continued on page 56...

Greetings, readers. *The Danger Room* is the place where my X-Men hone their incredible skills and are moulded into a formidable fighting force. See if you've got what it takes to survive a Danger Room workout by solving these challenges.

⊗ SENTINEL SQUAD!

Only one of the Sentinels opposite is **real**, the rest are just **holographic** copies.

See if you can find the real one by spotting which one matches the original exactly.

A

B

D

C

E

ORIGINAL

⊗ HERO HUNT!

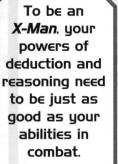

To be an *X-Man*, your powers of deduction and reasoning need to be just as good as your abilities in combat.

Show that you've got what it takes by finding each of these names in this word grid!

STORM   **CYCLOPS**   **COLOSSUS**   **WOLVERINE**   **BEAST**

JUBILEE   **NIGHTCRAWLER**   **ICEMAN**

W	F	H	V	O	S	W	M	R	O	T	S	I
I	C	X	N	Y	P	X	R	S	B	T	U	E
C	Q	D	H	W	O	L	V	E	R	I	N	E
E	M	K	T	E	L	X	T	B	W	L	N	L
M	B	S	A	U	C	W	U	S	A	Z	O	I
A	L	W	Y	J	Y	F	O	I	A	R	V	B
N	I	G	H	T	C	R	A	W	L	E	R	U
E	W	S	U	S	S	O	L	O	C	C	B	J

THE DANGER ROOM!

X TARGET LOCKED!

Think your aim is as good as *Cyclops* or *Iceman?* Study this picture for 20 seconds, then shut your eyes.

Using a pen, try to draw a dot on each target without peaking. *Good luck!*

X MUTANT MAZE!

Be on your guard, X-Men. There's only one safe route through this maze – take a wrong turn and you'll end up face-to-face with an angry bad-guy.

Can you work out how to get through without running into any of the villains?

START

FINISH

...Continued from page 53

ANSWERS...

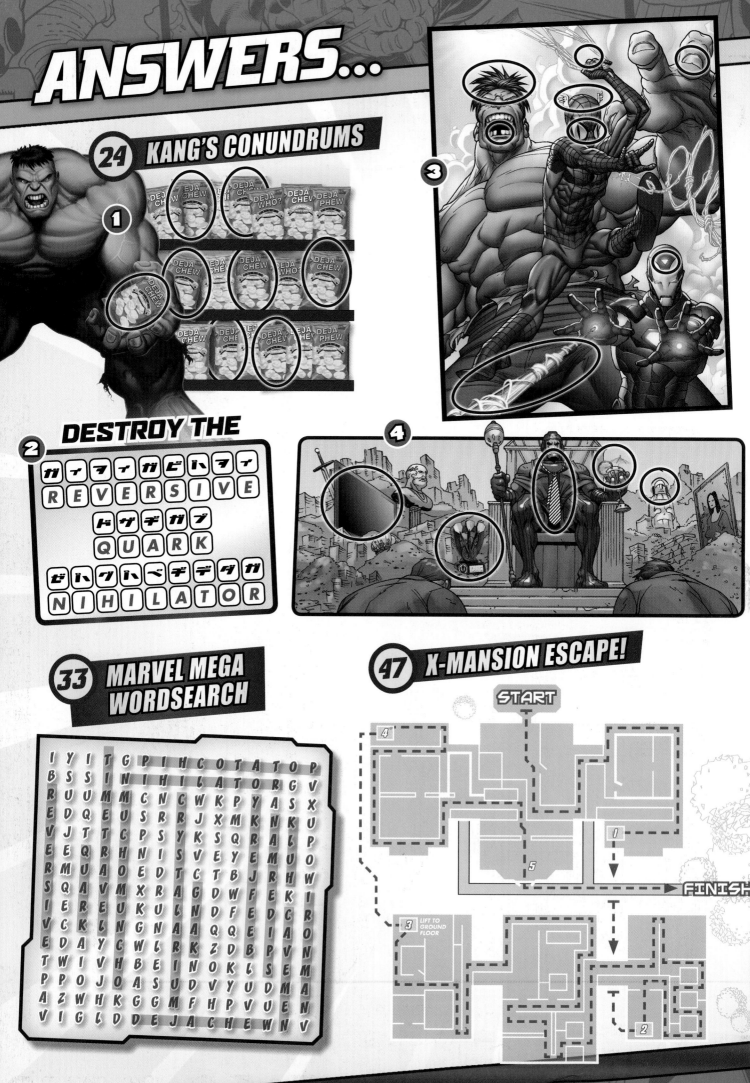

24 KANG'S CONUNDRUMS

1

DESTROY THE

2
REVERSIVE
QUARK
NIHILATOR

3

4

33 MARVEL MEGA WORDSEARCH

47 X-MANSION ESCAPE!

START

LIFT TO GROUND FLOOR

FINISH